FEET WITH THE JESUS

Feet

With

The

Jesus

by
Dick
Bakken

Dick Bakken (signature)

LHP

Design by Christopher Howell
Cover art by Abigail Rorer
Back cover photograph by Robert Turney
Typography by Maggie Checkoway Howell

Lynx House Press is grateful to the Oregon Arts Commission for the grant which helped support publication of this volume.

Library of Congress Cataloging in Publication Data

Bakken, Dick.
    Feet with the jesus.

I. Title
PS3552.A438F4 1986 811'.54 86-27625

ISBN 0-89924-054-2 *paper*
      0-89924-056-9 *cloth*

Lynx House Press books are distributed by Small Press Distribution
1814 San Pablo Avenue, Berkeley, California 94702.

———————————————————

Lynx House Press, Box 640, Amherst, Massachusetts 01004

ACKNOWLEDGMENTS

Some of these poems, sometimes in earlier versions, sometimes with earlier titles, have appeared in the following periodicals, anthologies, and other forms of publication: *Abraxas, Americas Review: Poetry of the Political Movements,* Anti-WW3 Internationalist Art Show, (San Francisco, Los Angeles, Tucson, New York, other cities), Arizona Commission on the Arts *Writers,* Arts Council of Fayetteville *Spectra, The Arts* Newsletter of the King County Arts Commission "Special Literary Arts Supplement," *Artspace: Southwestern Contemporary Arts Quarterly, The Bellingham Herald, Billy Goat, Bird Verse Portfolios, The Bisbee Daily Review, Bisbee Times, The Bisbee Wren, Book of the Cur: Dick Bakken, Poet* (Bev Walton video), Bumbershoot *Big Book* 8' x 16', *Calapooya Collage,* Carl Smool Rag Series #1 (textile monoprint serigraph), Centennial High School *Aerie, Chameleon,* Cochise College *Mirage, Colorado State Review,* Columbia College *First Run, Confluence: A Portland Anthology,* Dial-a-Poem (Portland), *Dick Bakken: Oregon* (An Emptry Bowl Video Production), *Earth First!, Editor's Choice II: Poetry, Fiction & Art from the U.S. Small Press 1978-1983, Encore Magazine of the Arts, Ergo!: The Bumbershoot Literary Magazine, Fennel Stalk,* Floating Poetry Gallery (Seattle), *Gold Dust: A Journal of Contemporary Poetry, Human Voice, Iowa State Daily, Iron Country: Contemporary Writing in Washington State, Ironwood,* Joe Uris untitled one-shot, John Dennis photo postcard, *Laundromat* audio cassette magazine), Leanne Grabel cartoon, Lewis and Clark College broadside, *Merlyn Gorky* postcard, *Mississippi Mud, Mr. Cogito,* National General Strike Day 5/20/70 broadside, *New Kauri, The North Coast Times Eagle, Notebook: A Little Magainze, Occasional Reader, The Only Journal of the Tibetan Kite Society, Only Morning in Her Shoes, The Other Side: Dick Bakken Live* (audio cassette), Pacific Lutheran University *Scene,* Phantom Gallerie Dog Art Show (Tucson), Poems & Pieces: The Reed College Dance Ensemble Presents Poems by Contemporary Poets (Portland), *Poetry Flash: The Bay Area's Poetry Calendar & Review, Poetry Northwest, Poetry NOW,* Poetry on the Buses (Pittsburgh, Atlanta, Detroit, Denver, Los Angeles, 15 other cities), *Portland Assemblage: Happiness Holding Tank, Portland Scribe, Portland Scribe* "Axis" Literary Supplement, Portland State University *Vanguard,* Portland State University *Viking 70, Prickly Pear/Tucson, Quixote: Northwest Poets, Red Hand Book: Collected Writings, Rio Grande Writers Newsletter, Salted Feathers, Second Bisbee Anthology, The Sierra Vista Herald-Dispatch, The Signal: Network International, Spectra,* St. Andrews Presbyterian College *Lance, St. Andrews Review, The Starving Artist Times, Star-Web Paper, The Stony Thursday Book, Stop the Butterfly, Suicide Notes: An Anthology, Sunrust Magazine, Those That Were There, November 18, 1972* (instant anthology), *The Tucson Weekly,* University of Washington *Daily* "The Matrix" Supplement, *The Vashon-Maury Island Beachcomber, Weed-Free, Willamette Bridge, Willamette Bridge* "Ash" Literary Supplement, *Willow Springs, The Written Arts, The Yellow Magazine, Yellow Silk: Journal of Erotic Arts, Z Miscellaneous.*

The Poem medley "Yes I Am!" includes the author's variations of "it's my soap" learned from Wayne Mabus, "feet with the jesus" from Lee Altman, and "eat bite" from Andrea McLean.

By the same author:

The Other Side: Dick Bakken Live (audio cassette), Brushfire Publications, 1986
The Coming of Spring (letterpress scroll), Carrington Press, 1986
How to Eat Corn (letterpress booklet), Carrington Press, 1986
Kazuko Shiraishi with Dick Bakken (audio cassette), Brushfire Publications, 1985
True History of the Eruption, 1980
Here I am (booklength poem), St. Andrews Press, 1979
Miracle Finger (works by children), Salted Feathers, 1975
Hungry! (new Bengali writers), Salted Feathers, 1967

AUTHOR'S NOTE

These poems, arranged here somewhat chronologically, were composed throughout two decades—from 1963, when I was twenty-one, to the present—and are mainly those that do not fit into my long-ongoing works in progress *Book of the Cur, Pinch Ass, Origin of the Valentine.*

Dick Bakken

for Carlos Reyes and Karen Stoner

CONTENTS

who does that old lady in art class
think she is anyway
asking me why i paint faces green
i'd like to paint hers
with a big brush
slapping it back and forth with both hands

and why didn't she like the crucifixion
was it because christ didn't shine
blonde streaming hair
because it hung tangled
matted with blood
because his jewface his
starved beaten body
twisted

i'd like to drive one nail
through her
and see how long
her hair stayed combed

VAN GOGH: CORNFIELD WITH CROWS

Crazed in thick air
of autumn's late afternoon,
he wandered without a coat alone
to a cornfield.

There, in a silence,
beating black wings rose slanted
to meet darkening skies. His wild eyes
stared after them

until the evening
air, light, rustled the cornstalks—
his shirt sleeves then filling whispered
follow, follow

TO JANE IN SUNLIGHT
WITH HER DAUGHTER EVE

I see Eve in your quiet eyes
reflect as you sigh and look to
your breathing breast. Its fall and rise

excite Eve's cadenced suckling cries
and they, your living smile. In you
I see Eve, in your quiet eyes

casting a mother's prophecies
—prayers for the first who draws through
your breathing breast. Its fall and rise

rock Eve quickly to sleep who lies
breathing with her first mother—you.
I see Eve in your quiet eyes.

Did the coming dusk shade her sighs
as our mother smiled looking to
her breathing breast? Its fall and rise

fell with dawn to darkening skies
—each breath counted time for life new.
I see Eve in your quiet eyes,
your breathing breast, its fall and rise.

It is midnight.
In the house on the sheets
naked, they sleep.
Her hand rests in his crotch,
his just loosely cups
her breast.
And nothing matters
but the moonlight rising
over their bodies.
In the next room her children
are also blessed
as the pale shine passes
under floated curtain,
glimmering
their uncovered feet.

WEDDING POEM

I don't know you, Teresa, but hear you are
glad and wedding your man today. I don't
know his name, but he must, like you or me,
be lungs and meat breathing around bone.
The spirit is born in the bone and flows
outward like hair, through the skin and on.
The surface is smooth. But when you love
let your hands press the bones beneath
his breast. Let your lips follow the veins
swelling his forearm. Let your cheek brush
the small hairs at his ankle. He is alive—
on both sides of his skin. Wed him pulse
for pulse. And you will never sin against
the bones and hair. Or against the veins
that flow in dark tangles from the heart.

THE LIFE MODEL

Bright as the green apple

thrust out,
light glistens her

wrist, shoulder blades, buttocks.

Swirls pinned high on her head
come wisping down . . .

All that shine! all over one body

and the silver
pin in her dark hair.

CONCERTINA AND MANDOLIN

Kiss me, sweet gypsy,
until I'm down dead.

Reeling with your men
over my bones, laugh

all damn night, spill
wine into tramped earth.

SONG OF THE PERSIAN CAVALRYMAN

Brighter than raised saber flashing,
   my dove, are your small breasts, brighter
      than polished buckler, spurs spinning at noon.

More than all my shouts are your shimmery
   bracelets and tinkling ankle-bell, the turn
      of your slender foot, unslippered.

More dear! than bugle and banner, than flying
   vermilion plume, is your floated veil,
      your dusky, falling hair, your clove sigh.

Redder than war horses galloping to close,
   sweeter, my dove, than heart's blood
      of the infidel, your two lips.

God:
What food
will you eat always—
if you have one choice only
and forever?

Adam:
The flesh of the apple.

God:
What will you
call the days when apples
hang red and gold
and drop from the limbs?

Adam:
The fall.

God:
And when the tree is bare,
what then will warm you and give you
light?

Adam:
The apple and the sun will
have been plenty.

AUTUMN

Two girls laughing
hold up their
hair, soap
each other's backs
pinched
and shoving.
Their guys walking
the woods for
elk, their loosed
hair bubbly,
they shriek together
sliding
to the tiles.
As they
roll under warm
spray, butts
and cunts drenched,
they squeal
slipping,
then almost
swimming. This
afternoon of red
they flood
till the
cold water comes.

5 A.M. XMAS 1968

She wades drifts
cross town in his coat, wind
icing her breast through one clean hole,
to his home, into his
mother's arms.

In the full closet
they wind themselves in
heavy, hanging, man-smelling clothes,
shut their eyes, and breathe
deep and long.

THE FEET

1
All day
her feet tied in leather
steam in their juice.
Tender and spongy,
by night
her feet ache with her heart
and lungs.

2
A poultice of garlic
and balm
on her soles:
in the morning she will taste
garlic on her breath.

3
In her slumber
she does not see her child
floating
near the ceiling,

whose hair shines
because today her feet
breathed
against the camomile flowering
over the mold and bones
of her father.

4
If her hands
rubbing her mother's feet
slacken
the cords lately gone stiff
through the neck,

then, lovers, place your soles
together as often
as your mouths
for their subtle mist
allows all our angels to shine
and fly.

5
In the hot bath
her calves let go of her ankles
and feet, their pores
open and her mind floats.

LEARNING TO MAKE PEOPLE

She watches the heavy sway
of his penis as he switches

his back with birch wands.
Mist rises from her belly

and thighs. They are gods,
the first two of us, ready

to make people. All night
under stars, they call up to

the heights what should be
good names, very good names,

then dash hooting to the
snow-fed creek and plunge.

As all dies

in quickening color and chill
into winter, rose-faced
lovers, frisking
old men and girls arm in arm

go walking

their glad dogs through the park
under branches ablaze
with the dying. All of it

falls and falls

past those wrinkling eyes
as their laughter
stays visibly
in the air. To the dogs

they kick apples

from among downed leaves. O!
the barking! the hearts! the air!
as they fall together

over and over

walnuts ready to pick up
by the handfuls.

PRAYER

His feet, slender and sure, ripple the meadow-grass.
Let her cool hands touch his temples.

She wants her breasts pressed with his breathing.
His neck shines black above his mauve gown.

He brings a zebra skin of roasted palm nuts.
O Lioness, place your red tongue against his heart.

THE HUGE HIGH ENGINES UNHEARD

1
So screaming high
over rice and peppers and that water
all ashine, the grocer, carrot juice leaked at both ends
of his mouth, can't bring up in his bombsight
the alleyway homes or downstairs
vegetable shop, one stooped dawnlit
clerk puckering to his onions and plums, drops
of pomegranet beginning the tremor
in such thin fine beard.

2
Night after blue night
as stars and moon shimmer down
his bed and garden, the grocer in blooming pajamas
sees the tiny grandfather and mother upstairs
dressing their schoolboy, hears
clean muslin rustle down like spinach
and sprays of new ribbon rising from black hair,
smells the bright sprig of parsley
outheld and trembling.

My god what's coming!

A heron. Great long neck
outstretched. Just floating down
on the invisible air
into marsh. Huge back and wings
lit suddenly blue with shine

as I explode by without crashing . . .
head stretched around
so long.

NOTE TO THE INSTITUTION (Spring 1970)

Reasons for resignation or termination
and remarks of value for the record of this resignation,
for use in preparing summarized information.*

*To fill my days wandering and and shouting poems. *Because
—good luck—I hear Basho, Blake, Thoreau, Whitman . . .
and so stumble out to greet them. *Because this indoor
light dulls my vision: no Professor has yet startled light-
ning from a desk. *Because each judgment I ink on paper
—C and B—makes me creep. *Because each pay hike and new
rank makes me smaller. *Because this junk factory loves
grade, rank, status, prestige, reputation, polish, cos-
metics, manners, money, property—O dearer than humankind,
our Milky Way, breast-Wisdom, and Truth. *Because the
whole carnivorous MACHINE is strapped together from here
to Vietnam: aie! Crazy Horse and Ho Chi Minh, these slick
elevators oiled up with blood! *My heart floods with Crea-
tion and the creatures of Creation. *Glory *be!* the Way is
lit, is good. *Beasts dazzle even the stars. *One living
buffalo, *one living Yellow farmer breathes more than all
the steel and paper in all Amerika's universities, culture
halls, and battleships. *It's time now to turn the page.

FIRST PARAGRAPH FROM "REUNION"

I was always making syrupy poems, dancing the bop, bumping into big girls' tits in the hallways, feeling under little girls' sweaters in their parlors. Fat Bessy had tits like cow udders, and the slick heroes joked in the john about a low-light party—dirty-bopping in the basement, bobbing for apples in ripe home-brew, five lettermen on a sofa, suds on their brows, Bessy laid out stripped and moaning across their muscled-up laps, all their hands and mouths kneading squashy flesh. The nice girls wore their chemises snug round their tail for the same daddy-o's—wheels, with their own jalopies, well-lettered prom kings, heartbreakers, smoothies and fox-trotters, who felt up the yell queens after the ball games, got in their tights, and hotrodded them home. I was too small and skinny, with just a twig of a pencil and no letters—just syrup—and the bop! Dancing the bop was for basement parties, or for skids at the Brite Spot—sweaty bike aces, greasers, kooks, niggers. But the little girls hugged me and sucked my ears, squealed like piggies with my hand in the wrinkle, steamed the glass in dad's old Plymouth rocking. And at the bad end of the ballroom I bopped and jived crazy man to Little Richard with skids and spades and let the slickers waltz off the girls.

MIDSUMMER'S NIGHT

Near the fire
grandfolks crowned in sprays
of oak shout and dance
with youngsters.

Pair after pair
the sweethearts hand in hand
leap the flames, flash
into darkness.

Sit up in your blanket and look and look. Who is he
in your bed? Is he Dick? Is he Ivan? He is a man looking
back through the dark. At Susan? Are you Susan?

You are a woman alive in your bed, awake in the dark
doing what a woman does. You look and look and wonder
where you are. In your room? on a balcony? in new grass?
in a graveyard? a tipi? And he is sitting up now too,
looking back, doing what a man does. He looks and looks
and wonders where he is. In an empty house? under stars?
in a dream? a ghostshirt? beside a woman?

Who are they, these two? They are man and woman.
They are sitting up in every field and house. They are
doing what man and woman do. They wake up as the stars
turn and they look and look and listen and bend closer
and look. And they are all good. They are good. They
sit up naked and look and wonder and listen and sometimes
they sleep smiling and whoever they are they are good
and crickets crawl in under their clothes.

THIS MORNING

This bright morning
at the grotto an old woman falls
into lily pads, startling
goldfish in front of the abbey, splashes
under twice swallowing muddy water
at the shocked father's feet.

Finally saved, sopped
gray hair to foot, vomit and lily petals
down her dress, she heaves low beast groans
and drips
as horrified sisters whisper
she is all right.

Now they all laugh,
a celibate wringing the slimed sweater,
her large family laughing now too
with their soggy, wide-eyed
old woman. "You fell in the pond,
Grandma."

WITCHERY

Wizard woman! Unholy
perfume! All your ethereal blouses!
With what sorcery you kiss
your toms and jennies, juggle
pots pans charmers, sweep about the house
with a broom. Out your window
are the midnight stars.

While brutes and their wives
rage on, dazzled apples drop into our
orchards. Gleaming,
the women, the poets, the deer
look up from the world
—bewitched!—and without leaving
sail all the fences.

BLUES FOR WILDMAN WILLIE

Walked in the Spokane
foothills where Willie used to shack.
Someone had smeared on a boulder
I hate you,
young lovers. Beware
lest you are damned
in this life and the next.
Heard an owl.
Back down on the avenue
met an old juiced wino who cried
home-made blues at me
all night.
Had my pen, jogged it all down.
Said way back '38 he jammed
with Hank Williams.
Now no guitar, but jerked up
his sleeve and fingered the chords
on his wrist pretty
as could be.

TWO WHITE DOVES

Such true darlings. We love
stretching naked and amorous before them
in our home new together.
How they adore us. O and each other forever.
Now watch me scrawl while they love
one moving hand. And when I go
for our first guest,
sigh it all to these two loves stunned
at your voice, your white hands
fluttering the page.
Yes then all you darlings, look up!
when I breeze in
hand in hand with Elizabeth.
For if you and I slide from her embrace
to pour wine, and she
kneels to these trueloves
smooching and crooning, ohh
they'll cry back
all the woos her lips can make.

TUMBLE SONG

When your tears and body
are dried and you are nothing
more than you are now—
a turning, a spinning
—When you are a ball of sticks . . .

I shall be wind, as I am
now, nothing
but a whirling, still rushing
with your rolling, bouncing bones
over the endless flat.

OLD BAMBOO FISHING POLE

Who we're bothered by
is that old gummer unsnagging the hook
from what's in his wasted hand. Not anything
he could swallow. Just what he's reeled
from this drizzletown slough. A squashed yellow bush
broad as his palm, stickers fanning out
like bones of something finished
long ago. I could leap
all over his puddle. He raises up the catch
for his blue eye
toward our great dim burst of light.
His back almost unbends.
You tell *me* what falls over his face.
He can lay down the pole.
He can go home.
Supper will be waiting.

HOW TO EAT CORN

My grandfather ate squash, ate corn. He ate corn
like this, lifting the ear, saying
You eat corn like this, when you eat corn
eat like this. And I pulled shuck and silk away
and saw the worm. On and on
as grandfather lifted ears and spoke and showed
his teeth and the yellow sun passed again and again,
the worm was curled under my thumb
only a shuck-width away, saying
This is how I eat corn. Like this. Like this.
I eat corn like this. When I eat like this
I am eating corn.

1

From her chamber Su Ch'in
can look as far as the River
of Gods. Five maidens comb
her hair and drape the fragrant
silk of her brocaded robe.

2

In a shallow pool beneath
the yews an old woman sponges
and turns her naked boy. She
wets back his hair and her sash
billows. His cap drifts away.

3

To a high thin leaf clings
one chameleon in magnificent
hue. Only its sides pulse
taking air. Not even a breeze
tremors through the grove.

4

Between the river and palace
in sweet-grass lies a young
archer sprawled in deep shade.
He does not brush away the
cicada quiet on his forehead.

CANTICLE FOR HER BEDROOM

bless fluttery Jo Ellen bless
her gait her song her white hands
on her face the door bless
the room
bless bless bless
the room all the light the air bless
bless the room the dove the lilies
bless her loving gaze
now only for Bill yes o bless
her white hands dropping combs bracelets rings
white blouse white
panties lilies bless the floor
bless her hands on her lips nipples cunt
o bless her closed eyes
her love coo bless her breath
bless air bless light bless walls brilliant
lilies doilies jars earrings perfumes book-and-coins
bless bless the turtling dove entranced
white feathers afloat air light
around her bless the room
she fills with joyous breathing
white feathers floating petals panties
bless her white hands what they do
her face held oh in his hands kissed kissed kissed
yes o bless tremors come all over them bless
bless Jo Ellen bless Bill bless love
bless hair eyes hands breath
breath breath
the room
light air feathers desire disarray
bless bless bless bless
pants pulled recklessly off
spilled pennies across the feathered
flowered unregarded floor bless
her bless her bless her
bless Jo Ellen

THE ANVIL

All day in the dust
the man and the dog and then the master
come in alone.

Where teams had trotted
the wagons, where the policeman stood,
the bucks sit with the does, the rabbits gather
and watch the rabbits, the rabbits
sit and wait.

When moonlight
rises to their teeth and eyes, your name
will be called and the wine
spilled.

THE BLEEDING

Your burlesque
is no good.
Yanking
all the curtains
like crazy.
Bashing glass,
letting
in the snow.
Sorry bastard.
She won't
come gaga for
you again
O in her scanties.
Wail through
the rooms.
You'll need more
than tissue
to sop
this up.
How your ripped
hands bleed!

Each room you
flail
gets a lace
of red.
Spatter wets
you lips and all.
Wheeze rosy
bubbles
if you flash
the bygones, if

just a bed
haunts like love.
O bang her
drawer
of panties all
to hell.
You poor
sucker, fall
down.
Take it
in a sliced
hand.
O you sap.
Let go.
You got it
all nasty.

Put your face
in those
hands, make
a whine
for torn gauzy
underthings.
Lose
a shoe kicking
the door.
Poor fucker.
Out back
nobody sees you
flop
choking
side to side

in scarlet snow.
You
valentine
O!

Open! just
like her
gagging O my god
with her love
boy. No
damn thing you
do can
stop those honeys
flopping
out all the
gulps
they want.

Get up. You
finished
your snow angel.
Lots of red
streamers
sputtering out.
Go wipe
that joker face.
Your heart
will spat
—if you won't
stop dancing for
her—all out
in such

gorgeous blot.
Hey now do
that Mardi Gras
stagger
back into the
ghost rooms.
O come on,
you sorry mess.
Blowing pink
froth.
Trying to
wrap yourself in
toilet paper.
In wisps
of panty.

Whooeee! big lumberjack,
what do you do when you get home?
You jerk the fridge and gulp
a beer. Oh so big
and hungry. Slap those buns and ketchup
onto the table beside
a pair of white nurse shoes.
But what do you do
when there aren't any weenies,
when there's a napkin taped to the next cold beer?
Jesus I'm sorry Bimbo.
Me and Oscie from the dimestore
left Tuesday for where
you ain't never gonna find us.
You drop that can and scramble the bedroom,
that's what you do. She's all gone
but those two white shoes.
And sonofabitch the Buick's not out back.
God your busted head!
all that spring in lay-up grinning nutso
with the nurse. Do you roar
through the house crying
your chainsaw into doorjamb and toaster?
Do you thrust the beer above your bent hardhat, pop it
with one squeeze, and weep
O shit as suds shoot down your arm
into the longjohns?
What you do is just stand and shake
all that ketchup into her shoes, twist the radio
high as timber cracking,
then sit and hold your big curly head.
Ketchup rolls out the eyelets
down her white shoes.
Oscar with his sunglasses is so far away hugging Lois
in your gassed purple Buick.
What do you do? What do you do, Bimbo,
when the beer you wanted is there, right there
between your two big boots?

THE TRUTH

This could be a true poem. But you
won't know. Not unless
you share a duplex wall with Larry and Helen
outside Tacoma.
There. Something made up already.
Not Larry. Oh you know that
when you see him on his birthday slam balls
to Mary Schnack in her tennis shortie.
Helen doesn't want to see. In just a robe she
downs one more swallow
by the hot oven and squeezes icings onto cupcakes
for each of Larry's two-dozen years.
If that snazzy little Schnack
even squats to tie his shoe, tell me it's black
and from there
we'll guess everything. Like Larry bounces
in after dark to get his birthday smooch and a beer.
Spread in a heart across the table—
all those pretty cupcakes.
You drank my last beer he says, lobbing a pink one
into the front room where it pops under
the couch. *Too damn hot in here,* as he snatches up again.
Hanging out in that robe!—
and he pitches one by one in there
under the couch. I could say slams with his racket.
But I want Helen to bang it on her oven like
Fuck!— Fuck!— Fuck!—
Not you he grunts wrestling the robe, shoving her stripped
onto the porch, hitting the bolt. And maybe you
could be telling the rest. No headlights, nobody in the yards,
Helen tight to the door whispering *Oh god*
Larry. Please.
I'll be good. I'll be good.
And she *is* good. Stretched snazz-up on the spread,

Larry naked in his black
rubber shoes, leaping over coffee table
to couch. Bouncing
above twenty-four cupcakes that'll harden there five months.
If there really *is* no duplex wall, no
Mary forever, how will you say what's happening next?
He prances past the Mixmaster— buzzing!—
Helen's robe flying from
round his neck. Onto the bed. Off. Back on. Squashes
fistfuls of icing
into his face.
I'm a big birthday bee! Falls onto her.
Bounces up over a night stand—cake pans—jockstrap—and back.
Here's my stinger!
Helen really *does* laugh. She wants to
love him. But can't. And
that's the truth. Even if there's no one to tell it.
Maybe Larry's birthday, maybe all these things
happen different days. Or not until tomorrow. I want—
the poem. It's all there is. But you'll have to
give me the true end. Please tell it now.
I'm standing here as lost as Larry.
And I need you. I need you.
I need you.

SATURDAY TENNIS AND SONATA

What a day! The guys
all in white
showing off sunlight. Blue sky
forever. And you go up
to volley—way back—in ethereal twist . . .
down hard wrong—*Christ!* You
won't be swilling suds with the guys
tonight.

Grimace the stairs alone. Raising a glass
of choice Chablis. To some Mozart. Your old tub
ringing full. If there's truly
elixir, it just might be
this *melody.* Hot water to the neck
and ticking away
through a cracked plug. Gaze into green vines spiraling
ceiling to knees. *Your* knees. Suddenly
your vines in shimmer. Out your open casement!—
white clouds like the guys sweeping
beyond blossoms
with the wine and adagio
into sky. And it's *your* sky, *your* white clouds
going rosy over dogwood. Breathe it all
in through the opened
blooms and wall,
through mist rising up the tendrils
from your chest as your
hands float
to sleep. This really
is your sleep. God bless your sleep.

Until you wake in dark
in the empty tub. Every tick and crescendo

long silent. Night blowing in
over your legs.
—You can't sit up. Now gasp to
twist. To lift. But you
can't— can't—
Must stare naked under vines coming down. Then finally
hear the distant voices
chorusing in.

No it's not angels. Just the guys
fresh from their suds . . .
hooting
as you strain toward their clapping hands—
No, really, guys! Goddamn.
I've been waiting for you.
Goddamn! Goddamn!

These are the names
of my horses
and sons. These are their names.

Mick. Max. Cracker. Mallory.
Hay-boy. Horace. Swish. Chip. Pippin.
Nicko. Dicker. Delmar.
Darlen. Spookla. Ambrose. Ross.

These are the names
of my daughters
and shrubs. These are the names
of my opening flowers.

Rosette. Betsy. Maribeth. Rosemary. Mae.
Moll. Holly. Heather. Belle.
Britt. Margaret. Pip. Pansy. Sarah.
Mary Sharon. Maud.
Arlene. Dawn. Rhoda.

These are the names
of my aunts
and great-aunts and these are the names
of my kissing cousins.

Olga. Iris. Eileen. Nan. Violet.
Lanette. Alice. Babs. Betty Jo. Lois. Flo.
Trish. Dixy. Roxanna.
Dot. Darlene. Floss. Fanny.
Pretty Pat. Squirt. Sis.

These are the names
of my bosoms and buddies.
These are the names and the names

of my road pardners.

Darlin' Bill. Lily. Dick-a-lick. Luther
Spook. Spiff. Sparkla. Martha Wong.
Johnny-the-Blondie. Indian Ronnie. Real
Grace. Jim. Jerusalem Slim.
Slam. Ghostman. Horseheart Nick. Chip. Okie
Mickey. Sissy. Rosio Cozy.

And these are the names
of my brothers
and lovers. These are the names.

Mick. Spic. Spook. Slit.
Slant. Wetback. Dyke. Cracker. Squaw. Scum.
Midget. Maggot. Grit.
Grunt. Slut. Lush. Trash. Spaz-ass.
Chippie. Nigger-hips. Swish.
Shitkicker. Dicklicker.
Darling. Darling. Darling.

YES I AM!

Are you a mouse
or a man? Yes
I am. Yes I am.

[*again, again, exuberantly*]

Rolling on the floor
laughing, my pregnant wife
beating me with a broom.

Yes I am. Yes I am.

O! the beautiful bombs falling!
Children leap as deer to catch them.
Mothers burst open like flowers.
Fathers spin away into orange air.

Are you a mouse? Are you a mouse?

Coming hard on
through the daffodils—
a Packard-full
of drunk grandmas.

Or a man. Or a man. Or a man.

O my happy son lifting
his arms in the bee swarm,
bees bearding his face!

Yes I am. Yes I am.

The poet the wild goose

in his arms! flapping biting shitting!
sprawl hugging through tide slosh
whooping to each other
ha! ha! ha! ha!

Are you a mouse or a man / ha!
Are you a mouse or a man / ha!

It's *my* soap
and *my* cock and I'll wash
it as fast as I want.

[*chant fast, then faster, faster*]

feet with the jesus / tail with the fleases
head in the bees's nest // up to wrong-doin'
slipper-chewin' / alleycat-screwin' piss blues

[*lickety-split*]

eat bite fuck suck
puff-a-nipple clit
titty cunt butt-bang
fingerfuck prick

ratshit batshit
slap-a cock twat
lard on a hard-on
snatch slick as snot

Ya yi! bombs falling like lemmings.
Haa! beating off all the poets with brooms.
Whooo! coming into daffodils.

O my happy son.

Are you a mouse!

Lifting his arms in the bee swarm.

Or a man!

Bees bearding his face.

Yes I am! Yes I am!

the poet the poet the wild goose

in his arms! flapping biting shitting!
sprawl hugging through tide slosh
whooping to each other
ha! ha! ha! ha!

ha! ha! ha! ha! ha! ha! ha! ha!

[*ha! through laugh awe jibe . . .
ending finally in croaked throat gasps*]

FATHER AND SON

Olympic Coast, July 17, 1980

On this point of rock—
I stand. Surrounded by breakers.
And cry out over them to where all of it
ends. Oh it doesn't curve much . . .
But it comes around. The sun
passing like love through my limbs. Rocks rise up
from the sea. Not so fast
as cedar lifting out
from them.
And I— I open— the one world
here. And let go my salt tears over
lips and breast. Right through these hands
into the inbreaking tide.
A gull cries like my grandfather dying
in my arms. The seal disregards
on a farther rock
fathoms crashing up. And an otter
rolls from under to behold—
out of a simple face. While ravens mock.
I call into their other
blue. Where a heron passing long as the vowels—
Though it goes not blue forever.
And the moon pulls round
with all there is. One bright Venus. Red
Mars. Jupiter.
Saturn. No it doesn't come fast . . .
But comes for me.
And here now
I cry my voice out into the breaking black.
And it doesn't go far. Or last long.
But it comes around.

ABOUT THE AUTHOR

Dick Bakken grew up in Spokane, Washington, and lived most of the first forty years of his life in the Pacific Northwest. He has taught at a number of universities and colleges, including Pacific Lutheran University, Portland State University, Thomas Jefferson College, and St. Andrews College. He has also been founder and/or coordinator of a number of poetry festivals across the country, including the Bisbee Poetry Festival in Bisbee, Arizona, where the poet has lived since 1980.

Dick Bakken would have no care at all for most of the above. His interest is in the magical, the transformational, the bardic, not in institutions or institutionally related information or institutional trappings. He is a poet entirely, a white glove full of winds and voices; that is what it is important to know about him.